HOW TO MAKE
MONEY ON

THE COMPLETE
GUIDE TO FINANCIAL SUCCESS
ON THE WORLD'S
BIGGEST AUCTION SITE

SARAH GOLDBERG

How to Make Money on eBay

The Complete Guide To Financial Success On The World's Biggest Auction Site

By Sarah Goldberg

Contents

Introduction

So what is the purpose of this book?

The purpose of this book is to help you understand how things work on eBay, how to be successful there, and make a lot of money. We are not talking about making fifty bucks by selling 5-10 items; we are talking about making thousands of dollars in months to help you get financially better in this difficult economy. eBay is a place filled with opportunities for you to take. All you need to do is read this guide to get a better and deeper understanding of the process and how it works.

This book will include methods of selling on eBay as well as several tips and tricks that will help you boost your sales. We will also include success stories that will prove the effectiveness of each of the methods and the amount you can expect to earn by following that method.

This book will also give you not only the basics of making money on eBay, but also discuss some advanced strategies. I'll also include my personal recommendations for other resources, including an **amazing** online course that can really help take your eBay earnings to the next level *(And I also have a way that you might be able to get the course with a huge discount. See the "Online Resources" section at the end)*.

We have all heard of eBay. Whether we know what it is or not, we have heard of it; if not from the internet then from the parody song by Weird Al. Must be popular, huh? So, what is eBay?

eBay is an online marketplace where you can buy or sell tons of different products.

How does it work?

eBay is a very simple and easy to use website. As a seller you have two options. When you put up something for sale, you can either put a fixed price on it or choose a starting price and let the people bid on it from there.

In *Buy It Now*, the first person who pays the full price gets the item.

In an *Online Auction* the bidding continues for a certain number of days, after which the highest bidder gets the item.

Why choose eBay?

eBay is not the only website where you can buy or sell items, so why choose eBay? The answer to this question is very simple and one you already know.

If there are two shops, one that has 10,000 regular customers with a 1000 new customers coming every day, and the other with 1000 customers with a 100 new customers every day, where would you want to put your own stuff for sale?

You are right if you want to sell it at the shop with 10,000 regular customers.

eBay is that very shop on the internet, except that instead of ten thousand users, eBay is said to have **300 million users** with at least **2 million** new visitors each day.

The ever-growing number of users greatly increases the chances of your stuff getting sold. Since eBay is a website that runs worldwide, even if the people in one state or country do not need something, there will always be someone on the other side of the world who will.

Another reason to choose eBay for selling your stuff is that you do not necessarily need to sell new things. While it is a great place for entrepreneurs or home business owners to start their businesses, it can also be used by ordinary people to sell both new and old things. You can sell your old and used household furniture, clothes, computer equipment, and even pet snails and fish, and much, much more…

The importance of eBay

So why is it important that you sell on eBay? In short, simply to **make more money**!

Customers:

Once you sell on eBay, you start gaining customers. The customers will not only see what they have searched for but they will also be able to see the other items you put on sale. This is free advertising and gives more exposure to your products whilst increasing their chances of getting sold.

Feedback:

The people who buy things from you can also leave you feedback or rate you, depending on their experience buying from you. If you provide good service, satisfy your customers, and manage to get good feedback, then that will encourage other customers buy from you. It will let them know that they can trust you and their shopping experience with you will not be a waste of time and money.

Trust:

eBay is a website that people already trust. The only thing you will need is to get the people to trust you as a seller. While it may take a little while to get started, once you have made a few sales and received positive feedback, everything is downhill from there.

Benefits of this book

After reading this book you will be able to:

- Sell things on eBay

- Get great feedback
- Acquire customers
- Increase the flow of your cash
- Start a business from your home
- Know what to sell

In the current declining economy, when people are taking several jobs to make the ends meet, eBay is a great opportunity for everyone to make money from home with only a little effort. All the work that you will have to do will be done from your own computer from the comforts of your own home in a little time. Of course, you will have to go ship out stuff to people who buy from you, but that would be it. There are no special requirements for you to start selling on eBay. A lot of students turn to eBay to pay off their student loans in no time. Housewives, stores that do not have enough sales, people who have lost their jobs, etc. have all tried and made money successfully on eBay. Occasionally you might come across someone who will tell you that you can't sell stuff on eBay that easily and that they speak from experience, but that is not the truth. The real truth is that these people did not sell stuff successfully because they did not know how to do it. So, in this guide, you are going to learn how to do it the right way. In the next chapter we are going to learn how to prepare and get ready to sell stuff on eBay along with some tips and tricks to help you along the way.

Chapter 1 - How to Create Your Listing

I'm going to assume you already have an account on eBay. If you do not already have an account, you can go to http://www.ebay.com/ and register one there. If you already have an account, login and we will proceed from there.

Your Seller Account

After you have registered on eBay you will need to set up your **Seller Account**. To do so, you will need to confirm your name, address, phone number, and specify a payment method. eBay recommends using **PayPal** so it is suggested that you get your PayPal account verified.

On the upper right corner of your screen you will find the **'My eBay'** tab. Click on that and go to **Personal Information** in the **Account** section. Here you will find your Account Type, User ID, Telephone PIN, About Me, Email Address, etc. Make sure that all the information that you have entered here is correct. If you want to fix something, click on **'edit'** and make the required change.

In the **Financial Information** section you will be able to select your **automatic payment method**. To do so you will be required to provide some additional information, after which you can select your payment method. The options you will have include:

- **PayPal**
- **Direct Pay**
- **Credit Card**

In our example, we will be setting up a credit card. On the top left, select **'Credit Card'** from the drop down menu and then click on **'Set Up Automatic Payments'**.

If your account type is an **individual account** instead of a **seller account,** then you will be asked to create your seller account first. eBay will send you a PIN via message or call you to confirm your number before you can create your seller account. You will be asked to enter your credit card information after your contact information is confirmed. Your seller account will be ready once that is done.

Note: eBay will charge you a dollar to confirm your credit card and will return it to your account once it is confirmed, though it may take a few days to do that.

Congratulations, now you are ready to sell stuff on eBay!

Creating Your Listing

You are required to create a listing in order to be able to sell your item.

Selecting a Category

You can either browse through the categories or type in the search box to quickly find the one you want. The **Recently Used Categories** shows the categories that you have recently used; this becomes handy once you start selling regularly. Make sure you select a category that best describes your item as this will increase your chances of selling it by making it easy for potential buyers to find it. Being vague with categories decreases the chances of your item getting sold, as it will become difficult for the potential buyer to find it. If you are unable to find a category that best matches your item then you might need to be more descriptive in your search.

You can also select a **second category** but that is optional. Some multipurpose items can really benefit from the use of a second category. Do not skip adding a second category just because it is optional. Having more categories means more potential buyers will find it.

You can also create a listing for your item from **similar items**. Since eBay is such a huge marketplace, someone else will most likely be selling something similar to yours and that means you can use those items to easily create your own listing. So once you select a category, eBay will show you some items similar to yours. They might not exactly be the same as yours but you can enter all the details to get the closest match to your item. When you find an item that is closest to what you are selling, click on the **Sell one like this** button. eBay will then automatically take some of the information from that item for you which you can then edit and modify to suit your own item.

Some of the items are associated with others. For instance, if you want to sell a book by another author then you will have to search with the ISBN to identify and add it to the list. Descriptions and other information for the items are automatically provided for items like these.

*If you do not find the item or category that you are looking for in the eBay catalog, you may add it yourself. Click on the **Add it to our catalog** button, provide some additional information, and you will be good to go!*

The Variation Listings

If you are selling an item that can be sold in different colors or sizes, then instead of creating a listing for every item with a different size, you can just go for the variation listing which will enable you to create just one listing with the options for different sizes or colors.

For Example:

If you want to sell earrings with precious pearls or colored stones in them, then instead of creating a listing for each color that you offer, you can create one listing and upload different photos to let people see the colors and select the one they want.

Similarly, if you are selling jars that come in different sizes then you can go for the variation listing and add the different sizes available and let the buyers choose the one they want right there from the listing on one page instead of creating a new and separate listing for each size.

Creating a Variation Listing

When you select a category, a pop-up window will appear asking you if you want to create a variation listing. The variation listing is not available on all the categories so if you are selling something that only comes in one standard color or size, there will not be a pop-up window asking you about the variation listing.

Adding Photos to Your Listing

You can add photos to your listing on eBay. This is also optional but it is highly recommended. No matter what you must upload a photo. The chances of potential buyers purchasing something that they cannot see are close to zero. Think about it and ask yourself whether you would buy something from an online store that you cannot see? The answer is no, you will not. Photos let the people know what to expect, especially in case you are selling custom-made or used items.

You can upload up to twelve photos for an item for free.

For standard items like books, movies, etc. eBay will provide stock images.

If you take your own images then you have to make sure that the images are clear and the object is clearly visible for the buyers to see. It is preferred to upload more photos taken from different angles so that buyers can see the object completely and get a clear idea.

For best results, take pictures in a room with ample light and a simple background. You can make the photos look better by showing the object in use. For instance, if you are selling a table you can show it laden with food with people sitting around so that the buyers have some more idea what it can be used for and what it will look like.

Tips for Taking Photos:

- Use a plain and simple background
- Use natural light instead of camera flash
- Do not edit the colors of the photo digitally
- The background should be clean, neat, and bare
- Using scales in the photos can give the potential buyers an idea about the size of the object
- Taking pictures up close for intricate items will put emphasis on the details
- Capture the objects or items from different sides and angles
- Show the items from outside and inside

How to Set Price for an Item

Now this part is really very important and tricky. Setting the price is not as simple as just entering the amount you desire, but much more than that. There are several factors that you will need to consider before deciding on a price. Sometimes people just want to get rid of an item and they may sell it for a very low price but we are working on making more money here. So, here are a few things that will help you set a price:

- Do not **overprice** - People are never willing to pay too much for an item that they can get for a lower price elsewhere.
- Do not **underprice** – It is a common belief among people, and new business starters especially, that you have to underprice your items to get started. This is not true and will only result in loss of profits.
- Find out about your **customers** – When you know who your customers are, then you know whether or not you can charge more. For instance, if you are selling an item like a second-hand television set or used home items then you probably already know that your customers will be people hard-up on cash or else they would be buying new stuff instead of used items so you cannot overcharge them. If, for instance, the item you are selling is a brand new Jacuzzi then you also know that your target customer will be someone who is not hard-up on cash and can afford this luxury. So that is somewhere you can charge more.
- **Uniqueness** – You can get away with charging a premium on your product if it is unique. If nobody else is selling that item, or not in your zone at least, then you can easily get away with charging more because the people will not have another option but to buy from you.
- **Research** – This is what will make you successful in selling. If you research and target a market, you will know how much you can really charge and make sales.
- **Profits** – When deciding on a price you must never compromise on profits. Your price must always include profit for you. The price should not be so low that there is a loss or no profit.
- **Popularity** – Popular products that are searched for more often will sell more than the less popular or needed items.
- **Compare** the price you want for your item with other similar items that are being sold to stay reasonable.

Fixed Price versus Auction-Style

Now for the pricing eBay gives you two options. You can either select a **fixed price** for your item or put it up the **auction-style.** Though I have already explained both before, we will go into a little bit more detail here.

A **Fixed Price** listing means that you fix the amount you want for the item and sell it at that price to the first buyer(s).

*The '**Best Offer**' option allows the people who are willing to buy the item to negotiate the price with you.*

Auction-Style pricing allows you to enter a price with which to begin the auction. Usually this is the price that is profitable to you. The buyers are then allowed to bid on it for a specific number of days and when that time is over, the item goes to the highest bidder.

The bidding is particularly helpful and recommended in cases when you are selling something unique or of a limited edition. You may have an original first edition of an 18th century novel that you do not need but there will be plenty of people out there who would pay handsomely to get their hands on it. Similarly there are other items like an autographed shirt, a signed poster, etc. that is rare and unique and would do well on an auction list.

There is also an option that allows you to do both fixed-price and auction-style on an item. In this case, the buyers can either purchase the item at the fixed price or they can bid on it, in which case the highest bidder will get the item, just like in the auction-style listing.

For best results, end your auctions on Sunday evenings so that plenty of people have time enough to see the item and bid on it over the weekend.

Shipping the Products/Items
The last thing you need to take care of is the shipping of the item. Shipping is not much of a hassle and most of the time eBay will offer shipping options automatically, depending on what the other customers who bought similar items chose.

You will have two options when it comes to shipping:

- Charge the shipping according to the size, weight, area, etc.
- Charge a **flat rate** which means that the same amount will be charged for shipping the item regardless of its size and weight or the area where it is to be delivered.

Free shipping is always preferred by customers. Sometimes the sellers offer free shipping, though they actually add the shipping cost to the price of the item.

In other instance,s sellers usually make the most money through shipping costs. They offer the items for a low price but charge more for the shipping. You can offer very low shipping but charge the customers a flat rate for it.

Chapter 2 – Presenting Your Product

You may be offering something unique and good at a very reasonable price but the thing is not going to sell all by itself. **You have to sell it!**

In this chapter we are going to discuss the ways that can make your item sell. Some people are unsuccessful when it comes to selling on eBay because all they do is upload the items and set the prices. They may be offering some really good packages but the presentation also matters.

People are usually careful when it comes to spending their money online. They will look at the items and if they see something off about it, they would rather pay a buck more and buy it from a different seller. So you need to make sure that your product is the one they buy.

Title

The title of your product should be something that best describes the item. The buyers will only take one look at it and that is your chance to catch their attention. Make sure you write a title that contains all the necessary information that the buyer needs to know.

Example:

If you want to sell a Panasonic television that is 24 inches:

Incorrect Title: TV for Sale

Correct Title: Panasonic 24" television set – Used

This way the customer takes one look at the title and gets the necessary information. When the potential buyers search for something, they will get a lot of results so they will likely scroll through the list.

Description

Okay, the title is good and you have the customer's attention, now what?

Now the customer will open up your listing for more information. The description should detail everything from the item to its condition and the things that will be provided with it like the remote for the television, cables, covers, warranty, etc.

Pictures

As explained above, the pictures will also show in the search results and if they are appealing, you will have gained a customer right there and then.

Policies

If you have any policies make sure the customers can read them before buying. If you have a no-return policy then let the customers know. Not being clear in your policies results in misunderstandings and leads to negative feedback from the customers.

Satisfying Your Customers

It is very important that your customers are satisfied with your service. Providing good services to the customers will lead them to tell others about you. When other buyers see the positive feedback that you have received then that will also give you a very positive reputation and lead to more sales.

eBay Success Story:

The story of Matt and Amanda Clarkson is very much a rags to riches story. Both of them left their school at the age of 16 and had been working but never making enough money, but today they are known as the couple who made £8 million on eBay. They did not set up huge offices or start with heavy stocks. Their humble start included selling from their laptop stuff from their home that they did not need and 2 years later, they ended up being eBay millionaires. In just a few months the couple went from the equivalent of $400 a week to $4000 a month. Now the couple averages about $75,000 a year. Below is some of their advice.

What is the most important thing?

"Give outstanding customer service. We decided to automate our business, something that is available as part of eBay. We've made templates of commonly asked questions so we just need to cut and paste. If your service is good you will get great feedback. People want to know that other people have bought your product first, and that they've lived to tell the tale!"

What is the big 'Don't?'

"Don't ever let go of the end vision of what you would like success to do for you. One of the biggest dreams I started out with was I wanted one day to be able to travel business class on flights and that spurred me on."

How do you retain customers?

"Build up a database of customers and email them teasers. With our kitchenalia category we send out recipe ideas and tips every month. For example we tell them what types of herbs you can use, and then suggest a new blender."

According to a recent survey, 95% of the people share their bad online shopping experiences while 87% of the people share their good experiences. So make sure that you provide good services and satisfy your customers so that when they talk about it, it is something good; it will help other buyers shopping with you by letting them know that you are real and reliable and that they will not be disappointed by shopping with you.

Chapter 3 – Selling Items You Don't Need

The most surprising thing about eBay is that you can sell almost anything. This is so surprising that most of the people can't believe it and therefore they miss out on the opportunities. They end up asking questions like:

"Who will buy my stuff?"

"Nobody will buy used stuff"

"I won't be making profits"

"I have never done this before"

"The things I have are in a really bad condition"

And a zillion more excuses. Yes, that is all they are: Excuses.

The thing is that when your target market is in the millions, the odds of selling are very high. Not all the people out there want brand new things. There are people starting out new business or those who do not have enough money to buy new things, and all they want is something that can get the job done. When people start out new businesses they are mostly on low or tight budgets. So instead of new stuff they just want something that works and gets the job done.

I once worked in the back office of an online store. Since the company was operating in the UK, I expected high-end computers, state-of-the-art equipment, etc. But I saw that the budget was tight and the company bought used desks, tables, and other paraphernalia online. So if you think listing used items will not work then you are wrong.

"I have a lot of items around the house that I do not need but which one should I list? What has higher chances of getting sold?"

The answer is simple. Whenever you are free, list the used items you do not need. Do not think too much about it because you are just listing the item and won't be running into trouble for doing so. If someone buys it, good. If they don't, no harm done.

eBay Success Story

Jenny Newcomer, a mother of two, had completed her education and had two degrees. Her degrees were of no use to her and she was $15,000 behind in her school loans. Jenny had a busy work routine and no room for another job. Already living on a tight budget, she was trying hard to not withdraw from the savings she had.

Like all of us, she also had splurged in shopping at one time or another and now had a lot of stuff that she should never have bought. (We all do, right?) But unlike most, Jenny decided to sell this stuff on eBay. She says:

"As I began to look around our house and clean up after the post-holiday madness, I realized how much stuff we owned. Bags, shoes, DVDs, books, iPods, old laptops, old kayaks, skis that didn't fit, bikes that we no longer in use, and the list went on for miles…

This was stuff we didn't love and certainly didn't need. So I started listing about 10 items a week on eBay. Some weeks when I had a few extra hours I'd list more and other weeks I didn't have time to list anything.

I kept at it, though, and slowly but surely things started to sell. Every time my PayPal account reached $500 or $1000 I transferred it over to put an additional payment towards my student loan balance. Little by little the amount owed kept going down. When I got it under $10,000, I was stoked and motivated. Over the next few months, I saw it decrease to only $5,000, then $1,000, and then before I knew it… $0.

Since I've paid off the loan, though, I haven't stopped! I'm selling more stuff as we speak to pay for plane tickets to Mexico this winter."

The one thing that Jenny recommends the most is to:

Check your messages at least once a day. Sometimes you'll get messages from potential buyers. They might want to clarify something or have a question about shipping and bidding procedures. More bidders mean higher end prices for you.

On getting good reviews/feedback:

After the sale, ship the items promptly and leave feedback for the buyer. Be sure to help avoid negative feedback (and honor the buyer's purchase) by shipping the items quickly after the buyer has paid in full. Normally the quicker you can ship, the more likely they will leave you a raving review!

Selling items that you do not need around your home is one of the best methods to make money. Though you may not need the item in your home, since they are home items there is someone else who will need them. The same method applies to office items. So if you still have a paper-cutter lying around that you no longer need or a study table you no longer use, go ahead and list it. You do not need it but someone else likely does.

So, even though there is no fixed success rate because the items that you can sell will vary greatly, one thing is for sure and that is that the sale rate will be very high.

Again, the key is to research the prices. You won't be making money if you try to sell a used item for the same price that you bought it at. When your target market is the people who are hard-up on cash then your focus should be selling more items to make little profits instead of selling a few items at higher rates. If they want to pay the full price then they would rather buy a new item instead. This method of selling home items is only a starter. In the next chapter we will discuss how to make more money by starting a business on eBay. There are people, like the Clarksons, who have set up businesses on eBay and are easily raking in millions by selling items. And they, too, started their businesses by selling the items from their homes and their offices that they bought, used, and were still in working condition but no longer needed or required.

Chapter 4 – Starting a Business on eBay

eBay is a fantastic place to start your business. The marketplace is full of opportunities for everyone. You can sell anything from used items to new items, things you make yourself or those you pick up from garage sales, etc.

Targeting an audience

The first thing you need to do to start your business on eBay is to decide what you are going to sell. Sure, selling miscellaneous items from home works fine, but when you want to set up a business it is better to start by targeting a certain market.

By targeting a certain markets, the chances of selling more items are higher. For instance, if you are selling office items and the customer comes to your page looking for a desk, eBay will show related items around it and he or she might just decide to buy a chair, too. In other instances, when people are buying small items they are more likely to buy several small items all at the same time, like a penholder, paperweight, paper-cutter, etc.

Buying Wholesale

There are plenty of places on the internet where you can order items at really low rates. If you order in bulk, you get even more discounts and save a lot on the shipping. Now you might wonder why people will buy from you instead of buying from wholesale themselves, right? There are two reasons for that:

- Most people do not know about wholesale
- Mostly wholesale items can only be ordered in bulk

This is what makes it good for you. One of the popular places to buy stuff at very cheap rates is www.aliexpress.com
Now most people who sell stuff on eBay aim to sell in bulk and you will be able to obtain great discounts. There is a sale with up to 50% off on one thing or another almost every day on Aliexpress, so one thing you can do is keep an eye out on the sales and buy in bulk when you see a good one.

There is jewelry, computer equipment, home items, garden products, etc. that cost more when bought alone but dirt-cheap when bought in bulk. These items sell for more individually because people can't buy in bulk. Nobody wants to get 20 pairs of the same set just to get it oat a lower cost. That is where you can make money. By buying in bulk, you can make money because you can:

- Charge more per piece (people will pay)

- Charge shipping on each item individually

So a pair of earrings that cost you $2 can easily go for $5 and there is room for more profits in the shipping.

Stock the items
Once you have the profits rolling in steadily, you should stock up on items. Do not offer any items that you currently do not have in stock. Customers want their goods in their hands within a few days after ordering.

One of the most common mistakes that some of the sellers on eBay make is offering items that they do not have in stock. Placing the order at the wholesale store after a customer has placed the order with you is the recipe for disaster. The wholesale people often get late with shipping, items end up broken during shipping, etc. **So, always have it in stock before listing it.**

Another common mistake that people make is they buy from eBay to sell on eBay. This thing only works one way, so if you want to make money, eBay will not be your wholesale store.

Marketing
Okay, you have a good shop setup and ready to go but no customers (or lack of them.)

Why is that?
Well, that is because nobody knows about your shop. What you need to do is market your products and advertise your page. Having regular offers and offering discounts to your customers also helps. You are more likely to sell something by offering a discount than you are by offering a low price.

Your eBay page can be promoted on eBay itself as well as external websites. This will bring you a lot more customers.

eBay also offers you the marketing tools to help you promote your page. These tools can be found on the **Marketing Tools** page. They include:

- Customized listing header
- Promotional flyers
- Cross-promotions
- RSS feeds

You need to make the most of these tools to get your page noticed.

Search Engine Optimization
The description on your products should be Search Engine Optimized so that the chances of your products ending up higher in the search results are increased. Following are the things that will help you get your products up in the results:

- Content
- Links & Link Popularity
- URL Structures
- Meta Tags
- Image ALT Tags

You can visit the following page to get more details on all the points mentioned above:
http://pages.ebay.com/education/SEO-introduction/

The most important thing is getting the keywords right. If there are too many keywords, the search engine will mark the post as spam. **The keyword density should be less than 3%.** That means that the keyword should only appear once in a 100 words. You can use up to 3 different keywords in every 100 words. The key is to use different yet relevant keywords. The keywords that you use should not be too vague or general. Use the 3 keywords that are all related to each other. People are less likely to get the results they want if they try single word searches, therefore your chances of being found are decreased. If you use multiple and relevant keywords, your chances of being found are increased.

If a person is looking for a keyboard cover, they will not be finding one just by typing '**keyboard**' or **'cover'** in the search because the results will include keyboards or covers for all things from remotes to cars. However, if they are specific and search with appropriate keywords then they will get results. Searching for **'Black Keyboard Cover'** is more likely to find them what they want. Therefore, make sure that your descriptions contain all the relevant words.

Avoid the use of:
- Single words
- Broad and unfocused words
- Words that are too specialized
- Unpopular words

Find more about **Search Engine Optimization** at:

http://www.hongkiat.com/blog/beginners-guide-to-seo-best-practices-part-13/

Chapter 5 – Research

We saved the best topic for last. Research is the most important part of making money on eBay. If you plan to set up a business on eBay then research is going to be your key to success and money.

When setting up a business you will need to choose a product line. The question is which product should you choose? It is hard to just stick to selling one type of item because the world moves at a fast pace. Something might be highly popular and in demand today but it might become worthless tomorrow.

You need to research and stay up to date on all the online trends and provide your customers all the in-demand items to make money. You can charge a premium when they are in demand and sell them at lower costs (without loss) when they are no longer as popular.

It is better to lower the costs to get the items off your shelves than to keep the prices high and wait for the one person who will pay more.

On eBay, it is very easy to find out what is in and what sells. eBay lets you see the **completed listings** of the sales. Stay up to date on them to find out what is currently selling and what is not. You do not need to waste your money buying items that do not sell or those with lower sales. Go for the items that have the highest sales.

Trends

Your research should include all the current trends. You can look for the trends on:

The Internet/Web:

The internet is the place where things go viral in seconds. No matter what you are selling, there will be websites and blogs dedicated to similar items. The fashion blogs on the internet have huge followings so if you are selling fashion items then you would do well by following the most popular blogs to keep up with the trends and know what's in.

Magazines:

There are magazines for almost everything today. You can find magazines for geeks, writers, fashion, architecture, music, games, etc. Almost all magazines have something featured in their **"Hot List"** or **"Top Ten"** section. These are the items that are either already in demand or will come in demand pretty soon.

The Television:

This one is a no-brainer. Most people have a television set and even if some people do not watch the TV, they do get glimpses of it here and there. The TV plays a vital part in promoting things. So TV should be a part of your research.

Newspapers:

Newspapers have entire sections dedicated to advertisements and promoting things. Though newspapers do not sound like much, they are highly powerful. They are sent out to millions of homes and whatever is in them is in!

Niche Markets:

Research and look into the niche markets and provide what the people need. Find out what the people in the market need or want and how badly do they want it. Find out how much will they willingly pay for it. Your venture will only be successful if you have all these questions answered beforehand.

For Example:

iPhones are a huge market in themselves and are highly popular. If you get into iPhones, you can sell a lot of different iPhone accessories ranging from iPhone cases to their speakers, protectors, etc. And this market is constantly growing.

If you embark on a venture without adequate research then it will be bound to fail before it is even started.

"What should I research about?"

If success is what you want then you have to research everything. Research what the market is, look into what your customer wants and how they want it, and find out how much they are willing to pay for it.

Holidays are also great opportunities to make money. Plan ahead of time and stock your items to be ready for the holidays. Look into what people said about the last holidays and find out what was hot, what people missed, and what they expect this time. Provide your customers what they want by being **proactive.**

Look into similar items to find out what the people are saying about it, what problems they have with that product, and how much they are paying for it. If you know how much a product is worth in the market before you jump into the venture, you will be able to estimate your profits.

Research the wholesale market to find out what they have and how you will be getting it. Oftentimes there are wholesale markets outside your country who will be selling original products in bulk at lower prices. The brands launch their products at different prices in different countries so a wholesaler in another country might have the same product at a much lower price and ordering in bulk would be saving you big bucks on both shipping and each individual item.

Research how to satisfy your customers because that is the only thing that will bring you positive and great feedback. If you do your research right you will know how important the customer satisfaction is. If your customers are not happy, you will be getting negative feedback which you need to avoid to keep the customers flowing in steadily.

Research when the best time is to sell your items. Find out when your customers get free time to be online. If you are targeting housewives then find out when they get their free time and adjust your auctions accordingly.

The auction listings do well if they end on Sunday evening,s as most people are free on Sundays. This means that everyone will have enough time to look at and bid on the products.

Conclusion

In today's declining economy, when people are losing jobs and have a tough time finding new ones while trying to support their families, pay the bills, and make ends meet, and those with jobs live under the constant threat of losing them, everyone is trying to find ways to make more money. While some people are taking up second and third jobs and exhausting themselves, there are other less stressful opportunities that can ease their problems. One of the easiest ones with a high success rate is eBay where people can make money by selling used items they have, as well as buying items wholesale and selling them as a retailer on eBay.

In this book we discussed different ways to successfully make money on eBay. The methods in this book were for everyone from the people who just want to sell the items in their home that they no longer need to those who want to increase their cash flow easily.

The first chapter in this book included the things that you must do in order to be able to sell. It included all the basics from creating an account to adding a credit card or selecting other payment modes, selecting a shipping method, creating a listing, as well as details about fixed-pricing and auction-style pricing.

The second chapter emphasized the importance of presentation, which is a very important aspect and can help you sell. The important points included writing effective titles and descriptions, taking good photos, as well as several others tips, tricks, do's and don'ts.

The third chapter was for the people who merely wanted to make money by selling the items from their home that they no longer need. It also works as a prerequisite to the fourth chapter.

The fourth chapter is for the people who want to start a business on eBay. It includes all the basic information as well as tips and material that will help get them started.

The fifth chapter is the most important chapter and is entirely dedicated to research and its importance. It details everything that needs to be researched in order to be successful.

The key elements to be successful on eBay:

- Research your market
- Know your customers
- Present your products well to make them appealing
- Pictures – A picture is worth a thousand words
- Offer as many payment options as you can – The more the options, the more the customers
- Be professional – Customers like professionalism and are more inclined to buy from sellers they deem professional

- Feedback – Make sure you get positive feedback from your customers because that will boost your reputation
- Buy items from wholesale – Sell retail!

Online Resources

While I have added as much as I could to this book, this is only to get you started and get the money flowing in. There is much more that you can learn to have a better and deeper understanding of everything. To be successful you will need to learn more about everything from how the eBay search works, the search engine optimization, what customers want, to promotion, making offers, and attracting and retaining customers, etc.

Video Courses:

One of the absolute best ways to learn about advanced eBay strategies is to learn by videos, as you can clearly see screenshots and visualize the exact methods to maximize your earnings on eBay. The best platform for online learning today is Udemy, which is an easy-to-use online education site. I have personally reviewed each of these following courses, sorting through the countless online courses on Udemy to recommend these as the absolute best courses to learn these advanced eBay strategies. Each of these three courses are very highly reviewed and taught by experts who know "the eBay game" and play it well with proven track records, so I am comfortable recommending them to you as **"must have resources"** to take your eBay earnings to the next level!

And here's the bottom line, right up front so that you can save time and get cracking with earning money on eBay: All three of these courses are really outstanding, but the first course here (Learn How Power Sellers Make Millions on eBay) is the best one. If you're the kind of person who likes to charge ahead and get started RIGHT AWAY, get this course and start your journey to success immediately!

Here's the last tip before I discuss these courses: Udemy often times has discount coupons readily available online. This site lists the most up-to-date coupons for Udemy so try one of the promo codes before you buy the course. That's my special gift to you!

Learn How Power Sellers Make Millions on eBay

Course description:

"Did you ever wonder how the eBay power sellers make their millions? Where they get their products? What products really sell well on eBay? This course starts with a simple concept: "How You Can Profit On eBay From Pocket Change" and takes you on an amazing journey into eBay, first with loose change and how profitable it is, then into the big top where you will learn advanced eBay concepts and finally how to master eBay!

How To Make Money As An eBay Affiliate

Course description:

eBay is one of the most used website online today, currently ranked at 21st on the entire web. Millions of people buy from eBay everyday, and we can get a commission from those people. With the top eBay affiliate earning millions of dollars every year its not hard to sell on eBay. In fact eBay sells 40% of everything that gets listed. Now I hope that make you think about joining eBay.

"I'll teach you more about how to create a powerful effective moneymaking website than your competitors will know in their entire careers."

Learn To Sell on Ebay

Course description:

 Been wondering what all the fuss is about eBay? Have things you'd like to sell but don't have time for a garage
sale? Think you'd like to try your hand at starting your own business on eBay but don't know where to begin?
If so, this course will show you exactly how to get started. The instruction will be entirely video-based. The first lectures will be normal classroom style, and then after that all videos will be views of the instructor's web browser with the accompanying audio describing what is happening. While this course has almost 2 hours of content, students should expect to spend significantly longer when putting the actual lessons into practice. The instructor will be available on a frequent basis to answer student questions, and live office hours will be held.

Helpful Articles

Following are some helpful resources that will both guide you and motivate you:

-   An article by Diana Fox on how she makes over $120,000 per month on eBay
http://ezinearticles.com/?How-I-Make-Over-$120,000-a-Month-on-eBay---Dont-Lose-Money-With-Wholesalers-and-Make-Serious-Money&id=3899961

-   Five great and highly helpful tips from a successful eBay seller
http://www.ebay.com/gds/TOP-5-TIPS-for-SELLING-ITEMS-on-eBAY-auction-/10000000001910734/g.html

-   An article by Matt Landau on niche marketing and mastering your niche
http://blog.weneedavacation.com/2014/01/10/mastering-your-niche-how-to-get-the-most-value-from-niche-marketing/

-   A must read eBay myth buster that will answer several of your questions
http://ebay.about.com/od/allaboutebay/a/Myths-About-Ebay-That-Need-To-Be-Busted.htm

- An article by eBay on ten important things that you did not know about eBay but need to know
http://ebay.about.com/od/gettingstarted/tp/eBay-Things-You-Didn-t-Know.htm

Further Reading

As I have mentioned in this book several times, your success depends on how much you learn and research. Following are five books that can be found on Amazon and will help you be successful on eBay.

How I Raised Myself From Failure **– Frank Bettger**

A business classic, How I Raised Myself from Failure to Success in Selling is for anyone whose job it is to sell. Whether you are selling houses or mutual funds, advertisements or ideas -- or anything else -- this book is for you.

Unlimited Inventory for Your eBay Success: Get your eBay business up and running with Unlimited Inventory **– Adam Ginsberg (Audio book)**

With this set "you will learn the tools of the trade, which will give you access to any product you would ever want to sell. This program teaches you how to acquire the products you want, whatever they may be. The program provides the potential to create unlimited inventory for your eBay sales and profits."

How to Buy, Sell, and Profit on eBay: Kick-Start Your Home-Based Business in Just Thirty Days **– Adam Ginsberg**

This is the insider's guide to making money on eBay. Adam Ginsberg is the most successful seller on eBay, moving around a million dollars' worth of merchandise every month. Not only will he impart his personal secrets on how to sell on eBay – learned through years of experience – and his tips on expanding your small business using eBay as a global market, but he'll also give fun sidenotes and anecdotes, keeping the book lively and making it a fun and interesting read.

This book will be a must–have for all current and aspiring eBay sellers, all small–business owners, and anyone who wants to learn how to start a million–dollar company.

How to Survive the Summer Slow Down on eBay! **– QuickSetLearning**

If you're trying to run an eBay business or just making a little money on the side, summertime on eBay can be the hardest time to make money with online auctions. This 2 hour seminar gives you a step-by-step guide on how to make a ton of money during the slow months at eBay. You will learn killer eBay strategies that not only will help you survive but thrive with your online auctions. Just a few things you will learn. 1. How to change your listing to make more sales in the summer. 2. What gets overlooked by many sellers on eBay. 3. The best products to sell in the summer,(you'd be surprised). 4. Three steps to skyrocket your summer auction success. 5. Turn your buyers into customers for life. 6. Discover 4 simple tricks that double your sales in the summer!

Starting a Successful eBay Business (Video Training): Start Selling Today – and Achieve Business Success Tomorrow! – **Michael Miller**

Best-selling author and eBay expert Michael Miller presents easy, practical advice and instructions for selling on eBay and launching a successful eBay business. Click play to follow along as Miller walks you through the steps necessary for eBay success... all you need to do is watch! LiveLessons is a six-hour video course organized into bite-sized, self-contained sessions—you'll learn key skills in as little as ten minutes! Each session begins with well-defined learning objectives and ends with comprehensive summaries, which help you track your progress. Follow along as your instructor shows exactly how to get great results in your real-world environment.

Excerpt From How To Make Money Blogging

By Sarah Goldberg

<u>Who Needs Money?</u>

Alternatively, perhaps I should ask who needs **extra** money. As the world struggles to claw its way out of the one of the worst recessions seen in years, people are finding it necessary to tighten their belts more than ever. Interest rates are at an all-time low, meaning that, while mortgage payments may be the lowest they have been in years, savings are sitting stagnant. Your money is going nowhere and there never seems to be enough of it to cover everything.

There are options. You could try to take on a second job, or even a third in some cases. However, some people are turning to the internet to try to earn some extra money. There are thousands of sites, all telling you how easy it is to earn money online, for just a few minutes of your time each day. Despite what you may read, it isn't very easy to make cash online unless you know the right way to do it. There are plenty of ideas out there, but not a lot of actionable plans to actually make you money.

One of the most popular methods for trying to earn money is through a blog. It sounds simple enough – you set up a blog site and start writing about a subject you love. But a word of warning - you can write to your heart's content; you can go on there every single day and update your blog with new information and stories but it won't make you any money. Why not?

Anybody can write a blog. Not everybody can make it work. That's the key – making your site work for you instead of you doing all the work and getting nothing in return. To make your blog work for you, you need to add to it – and I'm not just talking about adding more content.

The purpose of this eBook is to tell you how to make money from blogging. It's to show you no less than *5 different methods you can use* – all of them proven and all of them highly successful. This eBook is going to show you how you can turn your time and effort into money, **a potential goldmine** if you do it right.

Follow these methods and you will start to see money rolling in. You don't need to do them all at once. In fact, it is probably best if you don't – too much too soon will probably seem like too much effort and will have you exhausted. The trick is to start slow and build up your efforts and skill. Benefit from the knowledge of others, from learning how to turn a failure into profit and how to make your bank balance look quite a bit healthier!

Over the next 5 chapters, I am going to tell you, in detail, about each method: how it works and how to use it to its full advantage. I will tell you of the success stories, of people that have made money using each method and I will tell you how much money you can expect to earn in a month for each of the methods

Follow me as I lead you down the path to success.

Purchase this best-selling book on Amazon *today* by following this link!

Disclaimer

All attempts have been made to verify the information contained in this book but the author and publisher do not bear any responsibility for errors or omissions. Any perceived negative connotation of any individual, group, or company is purely unintentional. Furthermore, this book is intended as entertainment only and as such, any and all responsibility for actions taken upon reading this book lies with the reader alone and not with the author or publisher. This book is not intended as business advice and the reader alone holds sole responsibility for any consequences of any actions taken after reading this book; the author and publisher are not responsible for any monetary loss or gain that occurs as a result of following the methods in this book. Additionally, it is the reader's responsibility alone and not the author's or publisher's to ensure that all applicable laws and regulations for business practice are adhered to. Lastly, I sometimes utilize affiliate links in the content of this book and as such, if you make a purchase through these links, I will gain a small commission.